Ghost Writers
On The Rio Grande

by
Lynn Fullington

Rare Moments Press
2007

ISBN 978-0-6151-6613-1

Rare Moments Press
Rio Rancho New Mexico

In the aftermath of an historical event there are always unanswered questions but not impenetrable ones if you believe in ghosts. Ghosts, themselves, are a difficult question however.

This is a narrative of events in the history of the Rio Grande with three proper ghosts included, those of Miguel de Cervantes Saavedra, Don Quixote a La Mancha and Gaspar Pérez de Villagrá, a New Mexican poet-historian. All died within ten years of each other.

We know they affected these selected historical events just as they appear to influence events today as seen in separate poems interspersed throughout the narrative.

Ghosts must adapt to the times just as the rest of us must. Their skills as ghosts are a matter of growth and involvement. In this technological age we are just becoming aware of the resources they had all along. But that doesn't mean they knew how to use them.

Table of Contents

Ghost Writers On The Rio Grande

	Page
In The Aftermath . . .	3
Table of Contents	4
Canto I **Introducing Miguel de Cervantes**	6
Canto II **Introducing Gaspar Pérez de Villagrá**	9
Canto III **Quixote Restored**	12
Quixote, Alive and Well	
Evidence Scene I.	14
Scene II.	16
Scene III.	17
Our Way With History –An Aside	18
Unsung Heroes	21
Canto IV **The Chance Meeting Of Two Poets :**	23
A Tale As True As The Windmill Giants	
On The Plains of Spain.	
Canto V **How Villagrá met Don Quixote**	27
Over Awed By Such A Renowned Writer.	
Canto VI **Without Further Preliminaries Villagrá**	29
Begins His Story	
Canto VII **How The Poets Wait For Answers**	34
To Their Petitions	
The List	35
To The Death and Beyond	38

Brave Men Are Among Us   40

Canto VIII Telling of The Bravery at Acoma   41

Canto IX At The Risk Of Appraising   49
       A Non-Event

Canto X The Consequences of Believng   51
       Everything You Hear

Canto XI How Unaccountable Time Passes   57

Canto XII How A Noble Spin Came To Account   59
       For Complete Foolishness

Canto XIII How The Spirits Lost Their   63
       Rightful Place in History

Days Journey Of The Dead   65

Canto XIV Fortune Always Leaves
       One Door Open   67

Canto XV How The Lost Were Found   69

Canto XVI Two Honorable Gentlemen Travel   72
       To Chihuahua

The Uncertainty of The Raven's Call   77

Canto XVII Respect That Transcends Time   79

There Is A Song We Sing   82

Looking For a Vision Quest   83

Notes and Bibliography   85

Canto I Introducing
Miguel de Cervantes:
Bravery Into Obscurity

Yes, he fought duels
losing his right hand, and then banished.
It's a long story [1.]

Yes, he joined a foreign army
and fought Turks at Lepanto.
Captured on the way home by Barbary pirates
he was sold into slavery.
While they waited
five obstinate years for
Ransom to come from the Crown?
from the Family? from Anyone?
While year after year
he led prison escapes
for forty or more fellow inmates.

In chains on the dock,
his last stop was to be Constantinople.
There the ransom finally came through.
The kind of story one writes home about.
And yet he documented his trials before
Enemies used the Inquisition
to accuse him of dishonor.

Finally returned to Madrid
Never re-commissioned nor
pensioned with honor. Court
politics a bureaucracy out of order.

And so he wrote plays and a story
of a dedicated loser that inspired the world
Nobles took nicknames
from Sancho and the Knight
of Doleful Countenance.
But never knew the author
Nothing changed. [2.]
And so he waited.

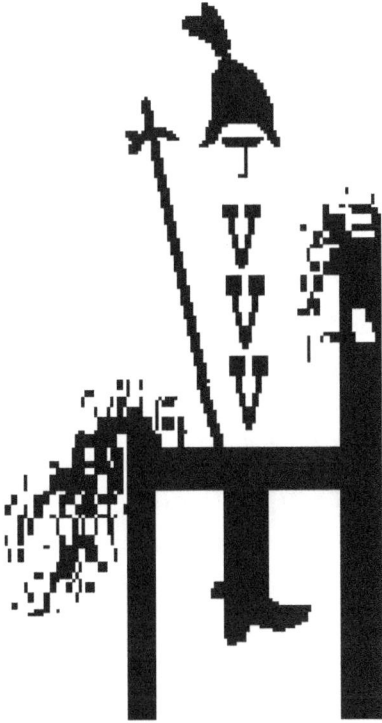

Canto II Introducing
Gaspar Pérez de Villagrá:
Bravery under Scrutiny

He was a captain in Oñate's Army
Those sanctioned by the King of Spain
to Colonize, save Souls in New Mexico.

A migration of families land hungry with their
cattle, their herds of horses.
Priests and noble sons eager for glory.

The King financed the priests,
Oñate financed all others.
While each man furnished his wagon
and armor if he had any.
And sat in camp year after year
waiting for permission to go. [3.]

Historia de la Nueva México was written,
even published but more importantly
This was Villagrá's petition to the King
for redress.

Actions taken in Mexico
convicted him in absententia,
banishing him, denying him all
government positions thereafter
As they did Oñate
for the fiasco
in Acoma
His was the glorious account
to set the record straight.

The hazzards of unknown lands
Made Villagrá the man who
found the water holes.

The man sent after deserters
who had stolen the horses.
He was the tracker who followed them
for fourteen days, followed orders.
followed classical precedent set by Romans
who beheaded
even their sons when
military orders were disobeyed.

Then without pause,
Villagra followed Oñate to Acoma
to fight the desperate battle
of reckoning on the sky-high mesa.

He leaped canyon gaps and restored
fragile crossings for stranded troops.
It was he who wrote these events
in verse, the very first history
of yet to be New Mexico. [3.]
Yet when he returned to New Spain
With prisoners he was too hot to handle.
Another commander was named.
He went AWOL to avoid the disgrace.[1.]

And voyaged across the ocean,
to gain justice in Spain.
As he wrote he glorified brave men
both the defenders of Acoma and
the King's men.

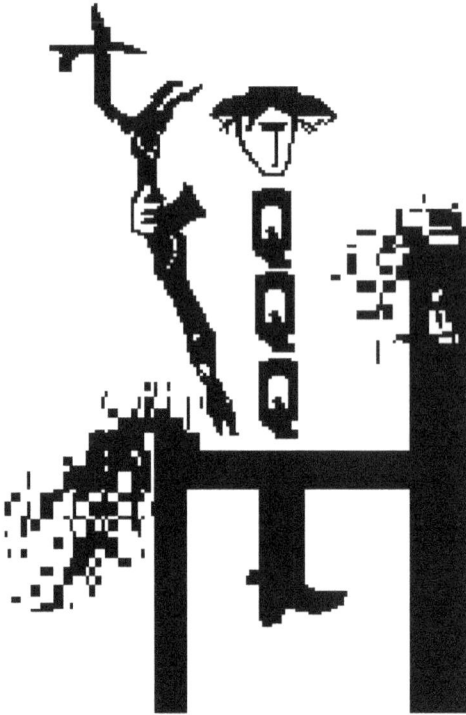

Canto III Quixote Restored

We call Don Quixote a la Mancha *Romantic* but
not *Nonsensical.*
His sudden attacks might unseat our logic
His insatiable need [7.]
to search out injustice,

To be dubbed a knight
even if one's armor be dented
left us in agony over Bosnia
Eager to pursue our quest,
Our lance lowered and charging.

Against a hidden army that
would not fight
Hoping someone would be left
to help us mount Rozinante
once more.
Nothing has changed.

The demise of Quixote was told
in the author's last book.
Pancho Sanza
Left at his bedside to grieve.
Yet Quixote is known worldwide.
His ghost carried across oceans
to mingle in the new World's history
But his poetry known to a very few.

Quixote, Alive and Well
Evidence: Scene I.

He was valiant, courteous and liberal
as any knight errant you might hope to see.
And there, a girl on the corner, a target
for midnight cruisers on a rowdy street.

"Wouldst care for conveyance
on this noble steed?
Better Savored than Sacrificed,

says the oldest of dichos."
Her mouth fell open in utter disbelief.
She'd said that this very morning,
to a lightly-used teabag
eloquently saved from the trash.

She could not ride with an airborne ghost
On a horse that lost all contact
with the rider on his back.
A dead tree branch for a lance.

Air currents lowered
the ancient knight's head
To his chest before restored
by his vigorous counter gesture.
An impatient knight
far too familiar with anti-gravity forces.

"You've got to be kidding"
She stopped to smooth
overly-solid, disingenuous hips.

***And wasn't it a shame
nobody played the game.
Yet myths taken for granted
On every street corner
all the same.

Scene II.
"You must not risk your virtue here,
gentle lady. Let me escort you:
A newsstand? A park bench?"
She saw kindness,
though the voice seemed a little thin

Man, that ought to be a laugh!
"Looking for a fight? Fine! the next cholo
will run you through.
There's no injustice here. Believe me,
I get paid! Only three nights a week
and I'm home with the kids.
You see old fella,
your kind requires
damsels in distress with really wet tears."

***And wasn't it a shame
they wouldn't play the game.
Liberal means there's no one to blame.

Scene III.

When the car slowed down, they called out
"How long are you good for?"
"Two hundred!" was all she would say.
Does that include the guy on the horse?
They laughed, honked, revving their motor
While she inspected spiked heels
for the damage they could do.

"Yeah, yeah." they opened the door
as the lowered branch came whizzing
through passenger, driver and conveyance.
Then over the hood and across the roof,
Quixote charged again and again
until all were exhausted from laughter
at the old knight's frenzy.
Those just passing by.
A free lance reporter, the off-duty cop,
the late-night social reformer

Laughter saves the valiant,
the courteous and the liberal once again.

***For they all stopped at Macdonald's
Yes, Virtuous and Villain alike.
Concluding Society was beyond their help.
The knight ordered "double fries"
and offered to share.

Our Way With History –An Aside

And how shall we confront history?
The part we are a part of.
With Doomsday Philosophy?
Reverence for a Judgment Day?
When all comes to an end?

Where is this monument
to the Unknown Dead Myth?

That nobody quite remembers ?
That mock grave so
that there can be
flowers and ceremonies?

The small box for the child's
turtle playing dead?
Until it actually happens
Is a glorious end?
This belief in a Judgment Day
begs the question

We who are the fearful
try harder.
Those who do not ask
are disposable.

Or shall we be Pagans?
Expect repetitions and recycling?
Like starting school in September
to learn better and pass on
to a higher grade.

Or shall we laugh at Man's effort to put
miscellaneous events into Linearity?
Somehow --- a Cause and Effect.
That just leads to irony
and a wry smile as we console
the bearer of the turtle box.

Atoms so small and skies
so big. Is there any sense
in asking for road maps?

Better to change the Firestones
and insist on a history
the way we wished it were.

The hundred men in a sunken sub
able to recount causes
a hundred different ways
But never had light to write them down.
And we will
tell their story
again and again
Sheer accident
would be too tragic
to succeed as history.

Unsung Heroes

The history of men
who would be great
starts on less glorious ground.
You would not recognize fate
in these small events, that happen
in turn to everyone. People who stretch
and yawn and turn off the alarm.
Who recall a hero on the way to the john

Wondering if this is their day
to save a damsel in distress
or defend a homeless person, say,
from monstrous trucks menacing
intersections. One does not need
a steed or a Toledo blade to be hidalgo.

Then comes the self-deprecating laugh,
caught once more
in Early-morning Childhood.
Damsels in distress will call it
sexual harassment;
The Homeless thank you
to mind your own business
or join them under the bridge
if you are so inclined.

"This urge to action, do gods instill it?"
Virgil has one of his heroes ask
"Or is each man's desire
a god to him?   For all these hours
I've longed to engage in battle
or to try some great adventure.
In this lull, I can not rest." [8.]

Yet days pass on endlessly until
someone notices a job
faithfully performed, for however long
despite downsizing and disturbing trends
of global warming. The honor belongs
to those with a will to endure.
They become heroes.
Often painfully obscure
in their last days.

CANTO IV   The chance meeting of
two poets : A Tale as true as the
Windmill Giants on the plains of Spain.

"And how came you,
Gaspar Pérez de Villagrá
A Creole of proud bearing
in your distant home. . .
(A curiosity in our one true Spain
Devoid as you are of pure Spanish blood)

. . . how came you
to write one vast history in verse.
How came the knowledge
of Greek and Roman heroes and poets
to attempt a petition - counting yourself
a son of this scholarly tradition?"

Villagrá obliged Cervantes in blank verse
as if in the introduction of an epic poem
In total seriousness, without hesitation
one foot forward,
gravitatious arm extended

"My noble parents wanted my horizons

broadened and sent me
to Salamanca and here
I learned all worthy things.
To return a true gentleman scholar
for our New Spain. Too young for that
I became a soldier
serving our two Majesties
Our boundless King, Our one true God."

"Then I must learn from you
about this new world,
fallen over the edge
of a very old earth." mused Cervantes.

"Surely you jest.
You know there is an endless ocean
that always stays fixed."
"How fixed? With that relentless roar?

A mathematician in Italy proves
there is one powerful force
but the masterly Galileo
does not call it God [9].
I have been subject to this
gravitational pull, myself.
No doubt Evil,
no doubt man-derived . . ."
trailing off with his whimsical smile.

"Please say no more,
you endanger us both!"
warned the serious new arrival.
Whether here or abroad."
You tell me you too have a petition pending?
If you are serious —such thoughts
must not be spoken"

"Ah yes indeed, very serious but
at my age in some New World place?"
Ah —-a bit of Panza creeps in---
But it need not be his island

There are positions in the Indies,
New Granada, Cartagena, La Paz
and Guatemala Are they near your country?
 Do you miss your homeland?"

"A thousand answers Señor
to your questions.
Should you allow
space for them to settle.

But where is this Panza?
I must meet him and Don Quixote
before I leave. This Knight of
Woeful Countenance. And why
Señor, do you smile?"

"Forgive me, but I would like
to meet the real Don Quixote myself.
He, too, longs for new adventures
and has petitioned the King
so let us meet again for your history
and his in Plaza Mayora or
Pino's — if you want
the second drink free."

Canto V How Villagrá met the
illustrious Knight Don Quixote and
Cervantes in awe of such a renowned
writer.

With swash buckling grand manner
Captain Villagrá, bold leader
of campaigns in New Mexico,
approached solitary Cervantes
sitting at his table tapping his foot,
tending his nachos.

"I beg of thee, most Christian . . Miguel?
You did leave me with that name,
did you not?
I come "to hear the song of arms
and the heroic men
being of courage, care, and high enterprise
of him whose unconquered patience
though cast upon a sea of cares . . "
I quote from my petition to honor
our historic meeting. . ."

"Good grief man, have a seat and pour
yourself a drink. You sound like Quixote
prompted you at the door."
Startled and abashed the stalwart soldier
pulled out his bench. "Where is our good
Knight?" carefully changing the subject
Searching among the shadows.

Cervantes leaned across the table
Was the Captain carrying on his joke?
It appeared he was not.
"May I be brutally frank with you, Señor
without risking your anger,
or your disillusionment?"
The Captain braced himself for the
jibes at his colonial origins.
"You are talking
with that pretentious knight,
or at least to the progenitor of his affairs."
The captain crumbled back on his seat.

"Oh what sorry business to live
with common sense that retaliates
on a most lovable fiction.
There must be some fragment of him.
Most likely here in Salamanca where . . .
then you are his author-- Cervantes?
Yes, this is your town!

How stupid of me not to suspect. . .
I am honored Sir, I am honored!"
And he stood again and bowed,
his eyes bright with wonder.

Canto VI   Without further
preliminaries Villagrá begins his story
in the most matter of fact language
with only a few additional literary
flourishes.

"Now tell me of your Nueva México.
And the prospects for a flinty veteran
like myself"

"Then Señor, you must know
your Knight's dented armor
will be essential. For there natives speak
unknown languages. There are
brave missionaries, with little time
to secure a Christian understanding
They care for souls that are innocent
but unsaved. Hospitality varies
village by village and sad accounts
of Spanish efforts to save souls
spread with the wind.
You never know who are the hostile

Yet they are a noble race.

"This history needs a long story to tell it
(found in my petition, Canto II)[3]
from the most elderly natives there.
About their ancient descent,
the coming and the settlement of Méxicanos who,
for myself,
think they did come
from the great China, all those who live
in the Indies. . ."

There must be a way out of this
massive recounting thought Cervantes
"Yes, there is surely a route
to China in all of this."
But tell me about the land, Señor, the land!
Are there Roads? Rivers? Mountains?
Is there Méxican gold?"

"Then you have heard the stories of Coronado's
Gold Pelicans?
Of the Seven Cities of Cibola?
. . . we have yet to see them."
Yes, There is a River
A careless turbulence that
rushes down to a high desert.
From mountain streams

and melted snow
And one day, past overcrowded cities
despoiled and merciless.

The water now is clear, chilled
and untampered with.

But with high desert comes heat,[4]
indifferent gorges that channel
the incorrigible river.
Deterred here and there by
obstructionist mountains
that are not impressed
by town meetings or debates
to negotiate with a river.

All fresh starts loaded down
with sand and silt.

Soon the great river
sinks from view.
To all appearances---gone.
Caught up in canyons
inaccessible to men.
Nothing to vote for.

And the struggle reverts
to survival without water.
No political wisdom supplants

the missing river. Needs?-- just
one. A simplistic yet nomadic
search for water.

Unexpectedly the river emerges
in narrow valleys
with a wealth of cottonwood,
and bovine grass lands.
The future for the culture by
which civilization is measured
The great river once found, again
is lost in a few short miles of time.

Men and horses have wandered for days [4.]
searching ahead for the water
Needed by the wagons that follow. At last,
throwing themselves on the water.
their horses drank till their skins split
or out too far, they drowned.

Yet no one seems to remember.
Years later they will search again
for the wily river that makes
civic virtue essential."

"And was your General so resolute a man?
In this wild and desperate country?"
Yes. But not without great forbearance
that encouraged deserters

Against all common sense
and military orders
a young soldier entered a native camp.[3.]
Through intercession
the General listened.
His execution was rescinded.
The unscrupulous took heart.

"Ah yes, queried Cervantes "What gives men the
will to be great?

These explorers think God gives the will.
The King the opportunity
It was Spain's Golden Age.

Then why should
a King so devoted to God's vision
legislate every aspect of a virtuous life.
Yet people evade their taxes and ladies
dance wontedly in the streets?
He does not bother to fund his kingdom
with roads and honest officials. Nobles
wear fine clothes and yet go
hungry at home where none can see.

When he loses our Armada and then Cadiz
He triples his prayers, redoubles his effort
but only to save souls'

*Canto VII How poets Wait for answers
to their Petitions and Court "business"
keeps them Spinning plans and Making
vows.*

As usual Villagrá could not resist
quoting himself.
"As little brooks in passing do refresh
their banks and make to grow
Whole graceful groves and clothe the same"

Cervantes listened with pleasure
to the unrhymed poet. He thought
It refreshing to hear of small efforts
that prompt great outcomes
from one who spoke of the great
disappearing river
—the noble Rio Grande.

"As you say it is the small mountain
streams that provide this turbulent Rio
and a lifetime of apt comparisons.
Then I must see this river"
resolved Cervantes.

"And I will meet you there
when our petitions are granted,
when next we travel.
Let me tell you
where we should meet ..."

Redress came but not as expected.
One petition granted, the other delayed.
The younger poet sent to Guatemala
As Alcalda to govern the region.
Yet Death came aboard ship [3.]
before reaching shore.
The older poet died of natural causes
not much later.

The List

For once, the gypsy fortune teller
was in a quandary
and posed the question:

Does one step back
and let nature take its course?

Or does one read the palm
in a respectful way, opening events
to unforeseen changes?
Quantum leaps were
not in her vocabulary.

From that day on.
Villagrá looked for probabilities
He was right to pose the alternatives
to Nature on a hot day
When he was hatless, and then again
to his Corpse on the day of his death.

With the first he was well advised
to raise his umbrella
and coat his arms with
45 watt sunscreen.

On his last day, he was caught
between the reality of "no answer"
And things his ambitious spirit
had left undone.

He looked in the mirror,
that auspicious day
But a ghostly image returned his stare.
Well, he could learn to exist with that.

He sat down and wrote a thousand things
to be done and for once
neither tired nor overwhelmed
by the magnitude of such a list.

The river must be straightened
so commerce reaches little towns.
Ships powered and the blue sky saved
from coal burning steam ships.
The Souls of Indians saved.
Their Gods as Gods of Classic
times to be saved
For stories around camp fires.
And how to meet Cervantes on The Rio."

The two ghostly figures
were left to roam at will.
Restless and unreconciled to their fate.
Yet destined to meet on the Rio Grande

The ghost of Quixote was already there
as seen in the actions of all chivalrous men.
Within weeks of learning ghostly transport
There was cheers and jubilation upon
the predestined meeting and
the three buckled their swords
and set out to travel through
pages of history.

To the Death and Beyond

And the good Lord never told us,
observed Cervantes.
Death was just a beginning.
A change of venue
but not with choir robes or halos
Or pitch forks and smoky fires
that never let up
We thought we were like
the grass and woods, the wild eyed
charred and sooty,
with only protective prayers
to put Hell's fire out

Then were we the brave ones
after all
who could believe
in living?
Maybe there is
some unearned bliss after death.
The bliss of total recall,

total knowledge relevant
with a moment's thought.
Secrets you didn't know you had.
All out there for your forgiveness.

Complete access to all times and places
Without waiting in line
Without Concords, without cell phones
Without computer chips, or radar blips
Without satellites
or any of technology's other step children.

God probably knew
but couldn't stand the boredom
without Death
to provide trauma
for the Living.

And of course dead poets
would understand the meanings
of any word spoken.

"If only we could write it down
all acts of brave men
and virtuous women.
Give our assistance freely
make changes substantial . . .
If only we could write it down

Quixote sang Sancho Panza's refrain
"Not to worry, What goes a ground
comes around" and he paused to
settle his barber's helmet.
"Even if it's all smoke without a fire"

Brave Men Are Among Us

Those who face danger and survive.
Many untried,
unknown even to themselves.
Consider those who cut life short
to perfect the prospect
of a life worth living.
Full recognition but no hesitation:
The Flying Tigers
in Burma.
The dog sled Explorers
to the North and to the South Poles.

And those the Villagra's ghost had met
defying their fathers
and the helmeted conscriptors
in Acoma.

"We swore loyalty,
they consider us friendly--."
Said the sons.

"They demand food.
We are sovereign peoples
Not bound by faulty treaties"
replied the fathers

"But father, they have guns
and horses —"

"We have the sky.
Who threatens the sky.?"

Canto VIII
Telling of the Bravery of Acoma

"It was hard to get used to"
Villagrá thought
"Starting anywhere, in any Age"

His comrades could ride
into the events of Acoma.

See the courage of brave men
in excruciating detail.

Like a movie he could not bear to relive
They would see the squad of soldiers
split up to follow the Acoma guides.
Each to a separate location
where food was offered --
but not forthcoming.

On cue came
the furious outcry of the crowd.
The Army Master stood waiting.
Calm with the patience needed
to prove friendly intent.

Yet the crowd waved their
clubs and lances much past time
to be courageous.
The soldiers rushed back.

Too late. Too late. And bodies fell,
wounds deep and fatal.
Limbs severed
Soldiers cut three times to the ground.
to rise and fight on.
Some jumping from
the mesa top to crash
on cruel rocks below.

When it was done, scraps of
fallen men were thrown down
to the waiting but powerless troops.[3.]

Survivors went searching for the General
returning from the peaceful villages.
He listened starkly, mourned for his men
and the fragile peace in this wilderness.
How many pledges of loyalty
would survive perfidy at Acoma?

When Villagrá found the General
haggard and aggrieved
He was consulting the priests
on the Legality of a War.[3.]

The effect on the ghost writers
was to insist on a rerun.
Quixote sorely torn
between the next event
and tailoring sorry events just seen.
Cervantes inquired "But what can be done on
top of a towering rock
Only hallowed-out steps
for ascent? "

Quixote consulted his ghostly experience
"We have ways to unsettle the
warriors. We must see it again"
Villagrá shook his head, Cervantes had
yet to know their ghostly powers
but he knew Quixote's rash ways.

Without warning Quixote
started the sequence once more
They found themselves sequestered in
the crowd as before.
"When I give the word
raise alarm and fire your guns.
What No Guns? Then throw those pots
stacked on the ground.

And as soldiers divided
were sent their separate ways,
Quixote commenced the warnings and
heaved a hefty pot.

The soldiers thought it an odd
celebration Though the words
were not particularly encouraging.
"Jump, Run, Save yourselves
Brave Champions of the King
and of your God."

The crowd shifted to avoid the pots
but saw no pot throwers.
Fear of the Gods entered their souls.

While villainous Conspirators
hauled off innocent bystanders,
pondering whose pots
had been squandered.

With precious minutes lost
the sequence unrolled precisely as before.
Quixote was vexed and aggrieved.
Villagrá could no longer watch.
Cervantes asserted what was
on each spirit's mind.
"Your General Oñate must take swift
and unrelenting action
to rectify this disaster."

Cervantes could see no answer
and concentrated on shifting the scene
as Quixote had done
and they found themselves
resting by the river. .   .
But this did nothing to ease their minds

"The General must know
this war is unacceptable to God,
to our King in Madrid. For it is likely
reactions would spread
down river to all peaceful pueblos."

"To unseat Deceit, one can only destroy
the Deceiver" advised Quixote
with one of his best all time proverbs.

"Later the General did take us back
and we scaled the Mesa on three sides.
Villagra reassured them
 The battle raged for hours,
And smoke billowed out
as the village burned.
For all to see.
Those captured stood trial.
like all good defenders
termed terrorists when defeated.

Villagrá lamented again
the many comrades gone.
Spirits had accomplished nothing.
Brave men still dying needlessly.
But Cervantes would have none of this.

"Your men would not approve
being denied their glory. Would you rather
they died of starvation in the desert?
How could they go down in history
if they were saved? How great would their
salvation be in Heaven
without this courage on earth?"
(Speaking of heroes and martyrs)

Canto IX   In which the Ineffectiveness
of Spiritual Intervention is considered
. . . at the risk of Appraising
       a Non-event .

It is doubtful that spirits tire or need rest.
Those new to their ghostly condition
did not know that.
Like a leg that is missing
keeps on expecting to walk.
so they took resting positions.

"It is time to change all of this!"
exclaimed Quixote. "Fellow Spirits--
we can still sail across the moon,
howl in empty buildings.
Startle non-believers into fatal last acts
—maybe even
into first stages of believing

But first we must have mounts --
a horse, a donkey, or a dragon
of your own design.
to give respectability.

For I do agree that if we are to assist,
our actions must be more visible,
more clearly seen."

For Villagrá the response was instantaneous.
To see restored his courageous stallion
last seen impaled in a spike-lined pit.
clearly laid to impeed his search
for the General.

And there the valiant horse
stood without a mark.
Cervantes reconstruction took longer.
These last lean.years
there had been no great horse.
Then he recalled the prison escapes.
Horses provided and
Thus appeared
A fine horse, indeed.
And Rozinante at an earlier robust age
was no disappointment either.

Canto X "Let them eat Leather"
and the Consequences of Believing
Everything You Hear.

True to her earthly nature
Rozinante showed signs of attraction
to her new companions. They were
fine horses after all. She pranced sideways
flourishing her tail. Dashed toward
Villagrá 's fine stallion
and raced out of sight.

The three ghosts jumped to their feet
and followed in the direction of
fading horse beats. They noticed
the grass had lost its green and the air
was hot and dusty. Had they out run
the river's coolness so soon?

The desiccated trail revealed bodies,
dead of course, and emaciated.
Villagrá called and his horse
came ambling back

They regarded
the thirst-driven land before them
as bands of Indians carrying

their worldly goods
left the pueblo behind them.
"What is this?" queried Cervantes.
What is this gray dust
drifting along the road
dimming the distance behind us?
These unburied dead?"

Villagrá searched his new memory.
Nothing resembled this sorry road.
He projected forward
to times he never knew.
"Ah, this is the drought of the 1660's
Lasting for years
unlike anything ever known.

"Look to the future my friend
and see for yourself.
A period of disaster
even for people living by the river."
"Ah yes, I have it now
A terrible period with raiders
from the plains
Turning blood-thirsty
in their hunger.

But who are these two stragglers coming
down the hill?" Use the key word
 "strangers" or "travelers"

advised Villagra still fumbling
for his answers.
"For us," Cervantes muttered
"that's everybody.
Let's try being "real" and ask them."

"Hello, travelers. Where are you bound?"
The two looked at the three equestrians
without surprise. "Greetings"
answered the older of the two,
(older, but not by much.)

"We come from a Sorcerer but
he said nothing about you."
The younger, (at most a boy)
looked at his companion.
"You just stabbed yourself,
and nothing happened just as
the Sorcerer promised.
No cut, no blood
Maybe we are already dead
and we too are ghosts."

"The good Lord only knows" answered
his youngish Uncle.

Did you say "Sorcerer"
in this Catholic country?
Cervantes was intrigued.

Quixote looked around
for the villains or injustice
that deserved his chivalrous right arm.
While Villagrá looked down the road
to see if the two were followed.

"Yes, a German Trader from Sonora
stopped me in the loft after Mass
He gave me a strange
message I could not read.
Though it is true,
I can not read much.

Being pure of heart and devoutly
at peace, he told me I was to swallow
the paper to be protected from
physical harm for 24 hours.
I would return to the village safely."

Quixote knew immediately.
The man was enchanted.
"I have been so myself
and you Señor, are enchanted!
Was your Sorcerer a giant? Talking to you
through a window?
Did he have weighty arms
that gestured in wild, circular motions?"

"No he was calm, almost penitent
speaking to me, being a stranger.
My nephew saw him too.

God in his Mercy protects me
or I would doubt my sanity
after the Sorcerer
and seeing you three this same day."
"I saw him too, Uncle —but why has the
old one a barber's bowl on his head?"

Quixote could not wait to answer.
"A poor knight errant out of his times
needs armor no matter where he finds it.
Until his ship comes in."

"Not likely on this poor river" spoke
the uncle "The mountains desperate
for water, rain that never comes.
Never has the river been so low.

Villagrá interrupted with some urgency.
"Will you be telling your account of
the German trader to others? You
will be in great danger long past 24 hours
if church fathers hear of this."
"I told the priest of the miracle"
"Unfortunately, dear Innocent, the Inquisition
is active and I must warn you

how carefully
you must tell such a story
if you tell it at all."
advised Cervantes.

"You are pure of heart. The Good Lord
God in Heaven will protect you" Quixote
declaimed with great fervor.

CANTO XI *In which Ghostly Adventures Allow Unaccounted Time To Pass*

Warning the trusting souls of trauma
that comes with Sorcery
the offer of rides was
extended to the two
returning parishioners.

Who could resist travel by ghost back?
Certainly not those who had already
faced sorcery and heaven knows what.
Light and airy they rode
with sounds of hoof beats and familiar
landmarks passing.by.
Time was pleasant, neither fast
nor slow yet all seemed changed.

Nobody recognized them.
Only one small fire
Only one pot boiling.
The prodigals discovered their
hunger and approached
the community meal.
Friends and neighbors
moved in listless fashion.

Yet so thin, so aged.
Since only this morning?

"Then cut those leather straps
you use for your packs
and throw in your sandals of straw.
That is all there is to eat."

The two cried out
"How could this be?
When the day was bright and the air cool
this very morning?" And seeing
the ghosts riding off they ran after them
shouting--- This is the wrong place.
Where have you left us?
Are you Devils after all?"

Cervantes turned to Villagrá "Where you
pondering the future?
Is this how we arrived
years beyond their time?"
"I had such thoughts
but not to change the Times."

So Villagrá thought backwards
until the day turned bright
and the afternoon air cooler.
Who would have guessed
random thoughts could be so influential.

CANTO XII   How a Noble Spin Came To Account For Complete Foolishness.

They recognized the German trader
Partly by his leather shorts. Partly by
his suspenders. Partly by his lusty yodel
(On the other hand he
might have been Swiss.)

His companion following behind
looked frequently over his shoulder
"Softly Señor, I beg of you --softly!
A song like that
could shatter boulders
even if we escape your jailers."

He shifted his blanket to the horse
While the trader pulled off his shirt
to stay cool, then discarded it
on the ground in a crumpled heap.

This will send them on a false trail;
While we double back to walk
 by the river. Tie the horse loosely
 so he wanders away
when our talking stops.
Then he saw the three ghostly riders.
"Ah, Señors it is much too warm.
We are about to let the river revive us."
Quixote rushed toward him
with a storm of questions.
"Are you the Sorcerer or just
an Enchanter once removed

Forced to give the poor man
a paper to swallow?"
"Oh, dear God why doesn't
that story ever ring hollow?

Answered the trader.
"It's months since the Gullible One told
this story that had me jailed!"[4.]
My accent makes it clear
why reason lost its hold
The facts are completely innocent."

"You did not promise protection
if he swallowed the strange words?"
The trader sputtered his objections
`'Twas only the name of my famous tonic
that clears up relentless indigestion.

During Mass we in the choir loft
Faced his misery that became unbearable.
The more I pleaded for my cure,
the more he scoffed
until in desperation
I asked the Lord's Blessing
Then pointed to my mouth
and made great show of swallowing.

The poor man *ate the paper*?!!
I left the loft,
By then overwhelming.
And here I am
escaping months of jailing
and five men trailing me"

That very moment a cloud of dust
drew their attention.
The five riders sure of the mission's end
appeared to be out
for the joy of the ride.

The lead rider asked "Do you see
anyone by that old cottonwood tree?"
"Yes three odd horsemen in armor.
I thought such ironwork
was scrapped long ago.
"Look they see us—my God if
they have not lowered their lances!"

Surely you jest! No here they come!
"Then to the side and let them pass—
By Heaven! I can see right through them!
These are Evil ones. The very work
of the Sorcerer—
Men! Make signs of the True Cross and Ride!"

In their panic two fell from their mounts
trying to keep up with the others.
"Come Back! Come Back!" they screamed
tripping over their feet and stumbling badly.
While the Spirits ran through them
and over them with vengeful cries.
They rolled under the nearest chamisa
Covering their heads in stark terror.

"Don't forget to tell your commander
how you fell from your horses"
laughed the gleeful Villagrá.
And the much satisfied Spirits
rode back to the business at hand.

Canto XIII How Spirits Saved the Day but Lost their Rightful Place in History

The German trader stood in
an uncertain state between
aborted plans and
the incomprehensible reality.
His jailers had turned in panic
and become small dots on the horizon.

His companion had seen
the trader talking --to no one--
Surely the trader was demented.
Would never miss his saddlebags,
so now to gallop away at break neck speed
all medicine bottles clanking.

"Never mind," laughed Villagra,
"let him go while you follow
the River. You will
find others escaping the drought

And we will lay out
some Unfortunate's bones
in your strange leather shorts.
No other sign will be sought
declaring you
Officially Dead and Abandoned.
according to five riders
in mortal dread
of a full accounting.
of their Journada Del Muerta"

Day's Journey of the Dead.

How aptly named
this Journada Del Muerta

This sandy stretch a scant mile
above the mighty Rio. A cliff-high
desert forcing the river west
No water near this sandy stretch.
No fit place for wagons or oxen.
Still, it saved a descent to the river.

Oxen could make it
with wagons lightly loaded.
Men who rested and traveled
after mid day siesta
could make it
into the cool of an all-night drive.

Even Texas soldiers
once promised Spanish leniency
Until the poor fools surrendered
Still some made it
with little water and less pity

It could be done
but once started
there was no turning back

Like the missile range,
there now, there's no turning back.
White Sands and its progeny
of the Atom bomb era.
once more discourage travel.

How aptly named this
Journada Del Muerta

Canto XIV It is said Fortune Always Leaves One Door Open

Cervantes wondered if all
traces of chivalry had gone.
Service to God and King
Willingness to die, even eager
when it brought Honor,
and Salvation thereafter.

In Extremes, it led men to delusions.
In Moderation, to noble action
in a noble country.

While Books of Chivalry
had been his target
his own chivalry was not.

Such ideals were not to be abandoned.
Even petty criminals held such beliefs
So what happened in this New World?

His ghostly question brought
endless images stored
in his troubled mind .
Example followed example
of cruelty despite laws to govern this land.

The privileged view
of All History belongs to the Dead
but this was no blessing
--if no grand solution appeared

Could it be the great distances
from centers of Church and State ?
He could bear no more and cried out
"Show me just one man from these times
that lived in honor
and traveled the Journada . . .

The massive overload stopped
and one Castilian and one Anglo
name appeared for 1810
A certain Don Fecundo Melgares
and the soon to be renowned
 Zebulan Pike.
Cervantes wasted no time
appearing in their midst.

Canto XV How the Lost Were Found

No one knew where
the rivers were, what mountains
lay in the distance
And so they sent Lieutenant Pike
to make maps, make treaties
with unknown tribes
Record all flora and fauna
All fortifications and troops
along the way.

There may not have been cell phones
but the Spaniards knew.
Sending troops into not yet Kansas
to find him and bring him captive
to Santa Fe.   Pike's already
intended destination.

But they could not find him.
In all that territory,
they could not find him.

Until in desperation his men with feet frozen
in the bitter winter
Pike sent one man
to find Santa Fe. When help arrived
it was a troop of 150 men.

Cervantes observed the respectful
distance of the two officers. One
refusing to surrender.
One refusing to insist on prisoners.

Pike's men kept their weapons
But submitted their trunk
of documents for scrutiny.
In their shirts and ragged clothing
were hidden the telltale maps.
Already Cervantes admired these men.

Unlawful belligerents, perhaps.
These Americans escorted to Santa Fe
and then escorted once again
to headquarters in Chihuahua.

This time by Lieutenant Melgares,
who had not found Pike in 1500 miles.
The two honorable men Cervantes
doubted he would ever find.

*Canto XVI   How two Honorable
Gentlemen Traveled to Chihuahua.
These mostly True but Unrecorded
Events now Told.*

The two lieutenants were natural enemies
Each taking pains not to show it.
"We always fight foreign invaders."
And winter piled up the snow
while men and beasts struggled south.
At each small town
Melgares called out the townfolk
They held festivals,
dances, and plentiful dinners
for the strange Americans.

Cervantes introduced himself
one frosty night
when parties were over
and candle light flickered
on Pike's late night
journal page.
"I see you think the women
are handsome
but woefully subservient."

Pike searched the shadows
for the unexpected voice.

He could barely keep to his seat
or was he asleep
how could anyone perceive his thoughts,
See his writing?
"I know your writing
because it is now history
and I am a relic of history myself."

And this most unbelievable image
pulled up a chair displaying the confidence
of one who knew his host as well
as Pike knew himself.

"I am truly immaterial but
greatly impressed
with your courage and determination.
It is not necessary to cover your journal
Señor Pike. If anything,
I would help protect your papers."

"Then you are not some frost figure
floating in the air?
I must be too tired to think coherently.
I am absorbing folk lore
these people tell with such conviction.
—At least to strangers."

"Be reassured Lieutenant, this image
is new to me also.

But I was once a person fascinated
with glorious deeds by
men in my own century.
My contribution was Don Quixote
who often confuses reality and fantasy.
but noble is his
devotion to his ideals."

"I have heard of your Don Quixote.
Forgive me if I'm uncertain
about which side of reality you are on"
And then the candle blew out while
Cervantes remained
as visible as before.

A darkened interior with voices
in a space barely large enough
for one man's sleeping
did not prevent Melgares from knocking.
Or calling out "Apaches! Señor Pike.
We must prepare."

The lieutenant's voice came as urgent
as thunder across the eastern mountains
or pounding rain on a leaky roof.
So late at night the danger-ridden
voice left little time
for positioning buckets.

"Apaches, you say?"
Cervantes echoed the voice's concern
Too curious to absent himself
from the unwary visitor who entered.
"Who are these Apaches?"

Melgare's regarded the seated apparition
With the courtesy
he reserved for strangers.
"Apaches, Señor are nomadic Indians
who steal horses for a livelihood."
And Pike sighed with relief to hear
another speaking to this ghost.
"Come in, come in and tell me
what you see at the table."

Melgares greeted Cervantes cordially
More surprised that no-nonsense Pike
acknowledged this apparition
than at what he saw before him.

"Thank you for the warning
but my horse needs no protection."
Cervantes assured the speaker.

Both Lieutenants readily
perceived the advantage of
a ghostly Cervantes riding up and down
in front of the enclosure.

And that is exactly how it happened.
A ghostly patrol never before seen
confirmed the raven's call
heard by the early morning raiders.

The raiders dispersed in panic
except for one young warrior
seeking his Vision.

The Uncertainty of the Raven's Call

I saw the raven fly
Then sit on a nearby branch.
I heard his cry.
He was not my Vision.
I am therefore waiting
I therefore must wait
for my Vision
Not for that dread messenger.

Now is my chance
For many horses,
For display of rare courage
I am waiting
I am waiting
for my Vision

What is this riding before me?
Then is this my Vision?
So powerful
that all can see?
This man on a horse
in ancient metal?

A ghostly vision,
thin as the wind.

No, my Vision will come
only to me.
For my life protection
For my life wisdom
But when? It is not to be known.
All depends
on a warrior's courage.

Canto XVII   As in All Chivalrous Tales Respect Transcends Time and the Fourth Dimension As Well

When he saw the rider ride
through the cabin wall
he followed
but stealthily through
the open door.

They stared at one another
the Vision and the Vision hunter.
Each waiting
for the other's words.

"Are you life-threatening?" Cervantes
asked speaking
that instant language all ghosts use.
That all men understand.

"Only when my Vision advises me
Are you my Vision?"
Cervante's ample memory bank
made Apache ways clear.
Foreseeing the man's future as well.

Sorrowfully
he knew not how to answer.
Lorca's somber lines came to him
"amethyst of yesterday and
 breeze of the moment
 I want to forget them."[11]

Pike and Melgares burst through
the door exultant from the raid
Not a single man lost.
Not a horse stolen.
Thanking Ghostly Providence
they lit the last bit
of candle. The Apache
in the flickering light
heard Cervantes say

"Gentlemen Here is a warrior
in search of his Vision.
No harm need come."
So two met the one—
Somehow, each trusting
this improbable situation.

"These two men are on
their way to Chihuahua.
And need their horses.
This man needs horses

to gain his Vision's respect
It's life-long protection.
You could help one another"

Melgares understood
the advantage of silent protection
in the desert ahead.
"Then say we honor
his Vision and accept the loss
of a few sturdy mounts for now
but others must stay. Our journey's end
will bring him a greater challenge
if they are driven off
in the dark of the night.

For then we will be watching.
The young Apache nodded.
"If you are not my Vision
I will remember
talk with such men."

There is a Song We Sing

"When my songs first were
they made my songs
with words of jet.
Earth when it was made.
Sky when it was made.
Earth to the end
Sky to the end
Black Gan black Thunder
when they came
toward each other
The bad things that need to be vanished
The bad wishes that were in the world vanished
The lightning of Black Thunder struck four
    times for them
It struck four times for me" [12.]

I know my Vision is
waiting for me.
or this Song would not have come
at this strange moment.
Now it is my song to sing.

And the Apache warrior left
without further word.

Looking For A Vision Quest

A Vision Quest
Meant deliberate Deprivation.
Alone in the night
in some kind of Wilderness.
Hunger in as many nights
Braving eyes that watched.
Ready to spring
With no regard for Visions.

For those waiting a double Sun rose.
and Waterfalls fell from the trees.
The Wind became a breeze
saying "Now drink "

For me it was when the Traffic parted
despite my jay-walking.
Street Signs and Street Lights
meant nothing but counted
on Gravity's sudden release of

Vehicular movement
for their Significance.

The Vision had not come.
The Song lodged in my throat.
Back to the singular Sun
Where the Raven waited to ask me my name

Notes and Bibliography

There is only one first-hand account of these matters, that of Gaspar Pérez de Villagrá, 1610 The unexplained mysteries documented in our histories remain. Scholarly accountings are noted below.

[1] Walter Starkie trans. Translator's Introduction *Cervante's Don Quixote* New York: Signet,1964.

[2] John Ormsby trans. Translator's Introduction *Don Quixote* London, 1885

www.donquixote.com/english.html - 101k - Cached - Similar pages

[3] Miguel Encinias, Alfred Rodriguez and Joseph P. Sanchez trans. and editors of *Historia de la Nueva México by Gaspar Pérez de Villagrá, 1610* Albuquerque: University of New Mexico press, 1992.

[4] Paul Horgan *Great River. The Rio Grande in North American History.* 4th ed. Austin: Texas Monthly Press, 1984.

Many facts that are known are documented in Paul Hogan's book . The myths and superstitions of the times are also told, such as the account of the German Trader. But this poem does not pretend to stop with that!

Grateful acknowledgement is hereby made of his scholarship and literary rendition of these events.

5. Margot Astrov An Anthology *American Indian Prose and Poetry. The Winged Serpent.* New York: Capricorn Books, 1962.

6. Jerry Williams and Paul E. Mcallister Eds. *New Mexico in Maps.* Albuquerque: University of New Mexico, 1979.

7. Fredson Bowers ed. *Lectures on Don Quixote* by Vladimer Nabokov. New York: Harcourt, Brace and Jovanovich, 1984

8. Robert Fitzgerald trans. *The Aeneid, Virgil* New York: Vintage Books, Random House, 1990 Bk IX.

[10] Stillman Drake trans. Galilio Galilei *Dialogue Concerning the Two Chief World Systems* Second Revised Edition Los Angeles: University of California Press, 1967

[11] Federico Garcia Lorca and Donald M. Allen *The Collected Poems of Federico Garcia Lorca* "Useless Song" c. 1920's p.59

[12] Margot Astrov *American Indian Prose and Poetry An Anthology* "Song of The Masked Dancers"   p. 213

The End . . . For now

As you know there is never an end to History.

About The Author

L. Fullington started her career in the arts as a graphics student at the University of California, LA then strayed into the sculpture at Arizona State University and earned a degree in Art History. Always her thoughts were toward teaching in the Southwest.

A sequence of teaching and studying resulted in a doctorate in Instructional Technology at Northern State University and post graduate study at the University of Chicago. Marriage to a NY illustrator turned professor prompted more teaching between trips to Mexico and Europe.

Upon retiring she began privately publishing small volumes of poetry. Since 1996 she has had work published in poetry webzines including *Snakeskin, Pogonip, Free Cusinard and Southern Ocean Review.*